CLOTHES

by Jenny Vaughan

Macdonald

Factual Adviser: Noreen Marshall,
Bethnal Green Museum of Childhood

Editor: Barbara Tombs
Teacher Panel: Coryn Bendelow,
Sue Dobbinson, Mary Wilson
Designer: Sally Boothroyd
Production: Rosemary Bishop

Illustrations
Lynn Breeze 6–7, 8–9, 10–11, 18–19, 26–27
Peter Bull 14–15, 22–23, 24–25, 28–29
Anna Hancock 6–7, 8–9, 10–11, 14–15, 18–19,
22–23, 24–25 (insets only)
Elaine Mills 12–13, 16–17, 20–21

'Happiness' from *When we were very young*
by A.A. Milne, is reprinted by permission
of Methuen Children's Books and the Canadian
Publishers, McClelland and Stewart, Toronto.

A MACDONALD BOOK

© Macdonald & Co (Publishers) Ltd 1987

First published in Great Britain in 1987 by
Macdonald & Co (Publishers) Ltd
London & Sydney
A BPCC plc company

Printed in Great Britain by
Purnell Book Production Ltd
Member of the BPCC Group

Macdonald & Co (Publishers) Ltd
Greater London House
Hampstead Road
London NW1 7QX

British Library Cataloguing in Publication Data
Vaughan, Jennifer
    Clothes.—(Allsorts ; 1).
    1. Clothing and dress—History—
    Juvenile literature
    I. Title   II. Series
    646'.3'09   GT518
    ISBN 0-356-13452-0
    ISBN 0-356-13784-8 Pbk

How to use this book

First look at the contents page opposite, to see if the subject you want is there. For instance, if you want to find out about clothes for children, you will find the information on pages 16 and 17. At the end of the book you will find a word list. This explains some of the more difficult words found in this book. There is also an index. Use it if you want to find out about one particular thing. For instance if you want to find out about umbrellas, the index tells you there is something about them on page 22.

CONTENTS

HEADGEAR

Headgear is what you wear on your head. It may be a hat, a cap, or a helmet. It can even be a wig.

Do you ever wear a hat? You may wear one sometimes, when it is raining. Or you might wear one to shade your head from the sun. Sometimes we wear hats to keep our heads warm. Some hats are part of a uniform.

Most of the time, people today do not wear hats. But things were not always like this. Once, just about everyone wore a hat. People thought you weren't properly dressed if you didn't have one on. They would have been very embarrassed to go out without a hat.

This pointed headdress comes from the Middle Ages. It was called a horned headdress. Some headdresses had just one point. They were called hennins.

In some parts of the world, people wear masks when they do traditional dance or drama. African masks, like this one, are famous. They are often carved out of wood or woven from grass, and brightly painted.

Try making masks of your own. Use card for the mask and decorate it carefully. Several people can make masks. Use them as part of a dance-drama. Some masks could show people. Others might be animals.

Hairstyles like this were the fashion in the 1700s. They could be a metre high, with wire supports to hold them in place. There are stories that mice nested in them.

Here are some interesting hats. But there's been a mistake. The hats are on the wrong people. Try sorting them out. Work out which hat belongs on which person.

Some headgear is made to be useful. Motorcyclists wear helmets. A helmet protects the head in an accident. The beekeeper wears a net covering over his head. Why do you think this is a good hat for a beekeeper?

THE TOP HALF

Today, people almost everywhere wear the same sorts of clothes. Mostly, we wear one set on the top half, and the other on the bottom.

On top, you might wear a vest. You may wear a shirt or a T-shirt over that. If it's cold you might have a sweatshirt, or a thick jumper. In cold weather it is best to wear several layers of clothes. This is because the air gets trapped between the layers of clothes and that helps you stay warm.

In hot weather we wear fewer clothes, made of thinner materials.

In the past, farmworkers usually wore smocks over their clothes. Farming can be dirty work and the smock helped keep the worker's clothes clean.

Peru

Japan

Morocco

Poland

Here are some of the tops that people wear in different parts of the world. People wear jackets, tunics, waistcoats, shirts and blouses.

Some of these tops have decorations and are worn on special occasions. They may have lace or embroidery sewn on to them. Others are simple clothes for everyday, woven or dyed in bright colours.

In the 1500s, women wore tight, very close-fitting tops called bodices. These often had big padded sleeves.

Men wore tops called doublets, which were also padded and embroidered, sometimes with precious jewels. Poorer people usually wore simpler clothes.

Children wore the same kinds of clothes as adults, Do you think they look comfortable?

Sometimes, there is a fashion for making bodies look a different shape. Men, women and even children used to wear corsets to give them tight waists and big chests. Try designing odd-shaped clothes yourself.

THE BOTTOM HALF

Today, both men and women like to wear trousers.

Things have changed. For hundreds of years, women in Europe always wore long skirts — even for work on farms or in factories. People were shocked when women first started to wear trousers. But in other parts of the world, such as India, and Persia, women have always worn lovely, loose trousers.

In some places, men wear long robes, or even just a simple cloth around their waists.

Here is a cardinal in the Roman Catholic Church. He wears long robes, as men did long ago. Other clergymen also wear long, flowing robes.

This woman is wearing traditional clothes from Pakistan. They are beautiful, baggy trousers and a tunic to match. This kind of suit is called a shalwar kameez.

Slops, in the 1500s

Trousers, in the 1800s

Saxon times – the 1000s

Breeches, in the 1600s

Around the time of the Romans, men in northern Europe wore trousers. Fashions changed, and men began wearing tunics or long robes. Later they wore puffed-out pants, called slops. After this, men began wearing breeches, which reached the knees. Modern trousers came after these.

A farthingale, in the 1500s

Panier hoop to make the skirt stick out in the 1700s

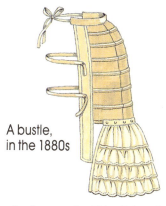

A bustle, in the 1880s

Here are some of the undergarments women wore, to make their skirts stick out.

These garments were padded, or had hoops of steel, whalebone or cane in them.

Bustles made skirts stick out behind. The women who wore these also wore tight corsets.

LEGS, FEET AND HANDS

Our feet can have a hard time! Without footwear, they would easily get hurt.

We usually wear shoes, sandals, boots or slippers. Most footwear is made of leather. Sometimes it is made of cloth or plastic.

Socks and tights keep our legs warm. They also make our shoes more comfortable.

Our hands have an easier time than our feet. They do not have to walk on rough ground. But they can get cold. In winter, we wear gloves or mittens.

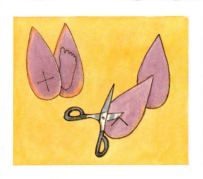

People in the Middle Ages liked pointed shoes. This is how to make some yourself.

Make a paper pattern. It should be a bit bigger than your shoe, and pointed. Cut out four shapes in cloth.

Cut a cross-shape in two of the shapes. Sew the shapes together as shown in the picture.

Turn them inside out, and you have two pointed shoes. Now decorate them.

This is what a running shoe looks like inside. It has soft padding to support the foot. There is plenty of room for your toes. Running shoes should be strong, light and comfortable.

This is a muff. It was made of warm fabric or fur. You put both your hands inside, to keep them warm.

On very cold days, you could put a hot potato inside the muff, to keep your hands extra warm.

This is a falconer, carrying a hawk. The falconer trains a hawk to hunt for small animals.

The hawk sits on the falconer's hand until it is time to fly off and hunt.

The hawk's claws are sharp, so the falconer wears a special, thick glove for it to sit on.

Moroccan shoes

Cowboy boots

Japanese sandals

North American Indian moccasins

Clogs from the Netherlands

These are traditional styles of shoes. People have been making shoes like these for hundreds of years.

The shoes were usually designed to suit the weather. Some were warm, strong boots; others cool sandals.

FRILLS AND FLOUNCES

Everyone likes to dress up. All over the world, people decorate their clothes and bodies. They may wear beads and bangles and other kinds of jewellery. They may wear feathers or flowers in their hair.

Clothes may be made of beautiful fabrics, such as silk and velvet. They may be decorated with embroidery and lace and with gold and silver thread. Clothes like these were very popular in the past.

Today, few people wear such fine clothes. But you can still see plenty of frills and flounces. The best place to look is on television! Dancers wear costumes with glittering sequins, and singers sometimes wear amazing clothes.

Silk is a very soft, beautiful fabric. It is made by the caterpillars of the silk moth.

The caterpillars spend their lives eating mulberry leaves, until they are ready to turn into moths.

In the past, men liked to wear frills and flounces, just as women still do. Rich men wore lace and silk and embroidered clothes.

Slowly, fashions changed. Men's clothes got plainer and plainer. But there are still plenty of men who like to wear fine clothes!

caterpillar

moth

cocoon

Then the caterpillars make cocoons by spinning fine, silken threads. These can be 1 000 metres long.

People then unwind the silk from the cocoon. They can then weave it into fabric.

This is traditional embroidery from China. The lovely patterns are sewn on to the cloth, using silk thread.

People all over the world like to wear jewellery. The Indian people of South America have their own kinds of jewellery. Both men and women like to wear necklaces and bangles. This is a man from Paraguay. He wears coloured feathers and beads.

This woman is a dancer in Thailand. She is wearing the traditional costume for a religious dance, which tells a story. In the dance, the woman plays the part of a goddess. Her costume is beautifully decorated.

CLOTHES FOR CHILDREN

A boy in the 1880s

Children's clothes need to be strong and comfortable. It's a good idea if they don't show the dirt too much. We say that clothes like this have been designed especially for children. This means that they are made to suit the things that children like to do.

You can design clothes for yourself. Start by thinking about the sort of clothes you like. You might want clothes for school, clothes for play or clothes for winter or summer. Think about things like the number of pockets you need and the kinds of decorations you want. Then draw a picture to show what the clothes look like. Now you are a clothes designer!

The North American Indians made cradle boards, for carrying babies. They were made from wood and covered with soft leather. They decorated them, using dyes and beads.

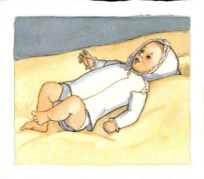

In the past, very young children all wore the same sorts of clothes. Both boys and girls wore dresses and petticoats.

Boys went on wearing these sorts of clothes until they were about five years old. After that, they wore trousers like adult men.

People used to think that babies should not move their arms and legs too much. They wrapped them in strips of cloth, called swaddling clothes, or swathing bands.

Children in many countries wear school uniforms. These are neat and comfortable clothes, just right for a hard day at school.

These children go to school in India. Many children there wear uniforms. You can tell which school they go to, by looking at the uniform.

SPECIAL CLOTHES FOR SPECIAL JOBS

People often wear special clothes to do their jobs. Sometimes they wear uniforms, like policemen and women, so that we can recognize them easily. For dirty or dangerous work, people must wear protective clothing.

Astronauts must wear space suits. It is very cold in space, but the sun's rays are strong and harmful. The space suits protect the astronauts. There is no air in space, so the astronauts must carry it with them.

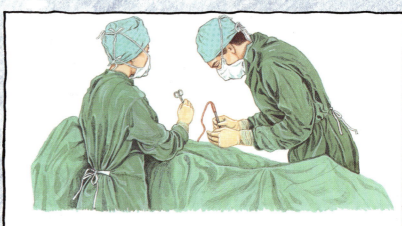

Divers under water wear special suits, to keep them warm and dry. They wear face masks so they can see clearly, and carry cylinders of air with them, so they can breathe. Flippers help the diver to swim more strongly.

When someone has an operation, they must be kept clean and safe from germs. The doctors and nurses wear special clothes. These help prevent germs from their bodies reaching the person having the operation.

Look around your home. Can you find any protective clothing there? The picture shows some of the clothes you might find. What jobs do we wear these clothes for? Try designing your own protective clothing.

Soldiers used to wear armour. It protected them from arrows and sharp swords when they went into battle.

Armour would be no good today. It is not strong enough to protect soldiers from bullets and bombs.

mask

rubber gloves

apron

Crop spray is poisonous. It kills insects. It could harm farmworkers too, if it got on their bodies. People using crop spray must wear special clothes to protect them. They wear masks to stop them breathing in the spray.

CLOTHES FOR PLAY

When we play sports or dance, we need comfortable clothes. We need to be able to move around easily. We need to stay cool. We want to look good as well.

There are different clothes for different sports. For dance and gymnastics, we might wear a leotard. Skaters often wear very glamorous clothes. These kinds of clothes are all made of stretchy material.

For rough and dangerous sports, we may need protective clothes. But these clothes must still be easy to move around in.

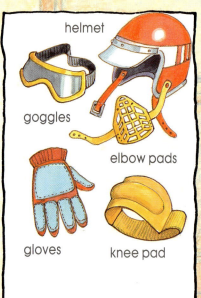

helmet

goggles

elbow pads

gloves

knee pad

BMX riding can be dangerous. It's important to wear a helmet, and pads on your elbows and knees. These are useful for other sports too.

tennis clothes in the 1880s

modern tennis clothes

Women always used to wear hats and long dresses – even for sport. This is how a tennis player dressed 100 years ago.

Today's tennis players are quite different. They wear short skirts or shorts so they can move about the court fast and easily.

Footballers' clothes are made in their team colours. They do not need the protective clothing American footballers have to wear.

Cricket can be dangerous. The bowler bowls fast and the ball is hard. It can hurt other players badly. Batsmen often wear masks and pads to protect their bodies.

American football is a very tough game. The players all wear helmets and padded clothes for protection. These make them look very big and powerful.

HOT, WET AND COLD WEATHER

All over the world, people wear clothes that suit the weather. In hot countries, people often wear light, cool clothes.

In cold climates, people wear woollen jumpers to keep warm, and jackets made of fur or filled with soft feathers called down.

To keep dry, people need waterproof clothes. Rubber is waterproof, so it is used to make wellington boots. Rubber was also used to make rubber-and-fabric raincoats, but they were smelly and heavy. Today there are many kinds of plastic coats that keep the rain off.

This umbrella from Japan is made from waterproof paper. You can use it to keep the rain off, and to shade you from the sun.

Do you have an umbrella? What is it made of?

One of the best ways to keep cool is to wear very few clothes. We may wear thin, cotton clothes when we are at home or at work. Swimming costumes are just right for hot sunshine and the seaside.

The Inuit people dress well for the cold Arctic winters. They have traditional clothes made from seal skin, with the fur on the inside.

They wear fur-lined boots and tunics, coats and trousers of fur. Women have fur-lined hoods and can carry their babies in them.

Happiness

John had
Great Big
Waterproof
Boots on;
John had a
Great Big
Waterproof
Hat;

John had a
Great Big
Waterproof
Mackintosh –
And that
(said John)
Is
That.

A.A. Milne

Fishermen need to keep warm and dry when they are out at sea. They wear strong, waterproof clothes, called oilskins. The hats they wear are called sou'westers, after the rainy south-west wind.

TRADITIONAL CLOTHES

In many countries, people wear traditional styles of clothes. This means they wear the sorts of clothes their parents and grandparents wore. Over the years, fashion has made hardly any difference.

In some countries, people wear traditional clothes for special occasions. They wear them for weddings, or for folk dancing.

But there are many countries where people wear traditional clothes all the time. In India, for example, most women wear saris instead of dresses or skirts.

This man keeps cattle on the grasslands of East Africa. He wears simple, traditional clothes.

In many parts of Europe, there are traditional ways of dressing. People often wear these clothes for festivals. This woman is from Greece.

Weddings are a time when people often wear traditional clothes. In almost every part of the world, there are special clothes for weddings. These pictures show a few. In Europe, America and many other countries, women like to wear a long, white dress. It is usually very pretty, with plenty of lace.

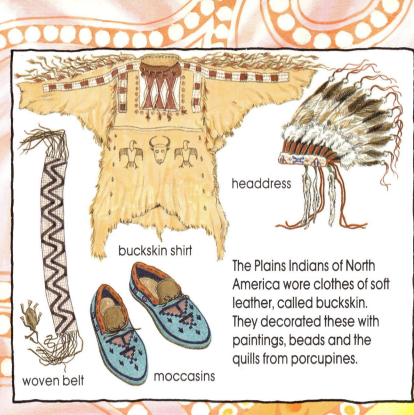

headdress

buckskin shirt

woven belt

moccasins

The Plains Indians of North America wore clothes of soft leather, called buckskin. They decorated these with paintings, beads and the quills from porcupines.

Sri Lanka

India

Czechoslovakia

Pakistan

GOOD-NIGHT!

When we go to bed, we usually put on special night-clothes. Some people don't wear anything in bed, but most people think it is more comfortable to sleep in something. We wear night-dresses or pyjamas. When we want to walk around the house in our night-clothes, we may wear a warm dressing gown over the top.

Not very long ago, bedrooms could be very cold places. People did not heat them at all, so they had to wear extra-warm night-clothes. Sometimes they wore socks and hats as well, to keep warm.

Night-clothes should be warm and comfortable. Children's pyjamas are often stretchy, with a fluffy lining. They sometimes cover your feet as well as your legs.

Some people like to sit up in bed to read or watch television. A bed jacket keeps them warm.

Babies spend a lot of time in bed! They also move around a lot, and kick their blankets off. This sleeping bag solves the problem. The baby stays warm inside it.

These are night-clothes that men wore in the past. They used to wear long nightshirts. They wore a dressing gown over these when they got up in the morning. Women wore warm flannel night-dresses.

People thought it was important to keep your head warm at night. So women wore a kind of bonnet when they went to bed. Men wore long nightcaps – just like Wee Willie Winkie.

Wee Willie Winkie

Wee Willie Winkie
Runs through the town,
Upstairs and downstairs
In his nightgown.
Rapping at the window,
Crying through the lock,
'Are the children in
    their beds?
It's past eight o'clock!'

THINGS TO DO

BEFORE YOU BEGIN

If you're going to do projects with clothes, you'll need something to work on. Collect as many bits of cloth and old clothes as you can. Don't cut anything up if someone wants it! You might find it useful to go to a jumble sale to find things for experiments. Make sure everything you use is clean.

As well as using the old clothes you collect for experiments, you can also use them as dressing-up clothes. Decorate them with frills and glitter if you like. You can even make dressing-up clothes from paper. Try making paper hats or a tunic from a paper sack, and then paint them in bright colours.

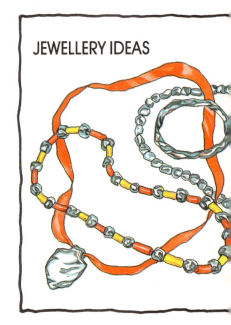

JEWELLERY IDEAS

JAM-JAR JACKETS

This is a way of finding out which fabrics keep us warmest. For this experiment you need a few jam-jars, all the same size, with lids. You also need some newspaper and several different kinds of fabric.

Use the newspaper to make heads for the jars. Give them all faces and hair. Then use the fabric to make jackets for each jar, as shown in the diagram opposite.

Now fill the jars with hot water. All the jars should be the same temperature. Put the jackets on the jars, and leave them for an hour. Then feel the water. Which one feels the warmest? Which one feels coldest?

Collect old jewellery – but make sure no one wants it! Or you could make jewellery. There are many ways you can do this.

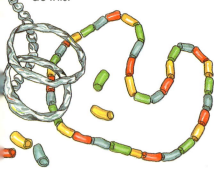

You can make beads from pasta, sprayed or painted in different colours. Or you can make beads from balls of paper or silver foil.

Silver foil makes good bangles or pendants. Use it to cover card. You could stick decorations, such as string or buttons on the card, and then cover it with foil.

FAMILY HISTORY

Look for old photographs of your parents and grandparents. You might even find pictures of your great-grandparents.

Look at the ways in which people's clothes are different from the clothes we wear today. Are the skirts that women wore longer or shorter? Was anyone wearing a hat? Was anyone wearing a uniform? What sorts of clothes were the men wearing? What did the children wear?

COLLAGE IDEAS

Use different fabrics to make a collage. If you put people in your collage, they can all wear clothes from different fabrics. Or you could make cut-out dolls of yourself and dress them in clothes you would like to wear. These could include summer clothes, winter clothes, best clothes and everyday clothes.

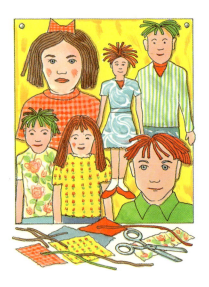

DYES

Have you ever tried tie-dyeing? It's best to dye cotton fabric. Choose an old shirt or T shirt. Use rubber bands and pebbles, as the picture shows. Now dye your shirt. You may need some help, as you will have to follow the instructions on the packet of dye.

In Nigeria, there is a special kind of dyeing. They paint a pattern on cloth, using a kind of paste. You could make a paste from flour and water. Use it to paint a pattern on a piece of fabric.

When you have painted the pattern, use the kind of dye you can paint on to fabric. Paint it all over, and let it dry. Then wash the fabric. The paste will wash off, and you'll be left with the pattern.

This kind of dyeing is a bit like batik. In batik, you use hot wax instead of paste. If you want to try batik, make sure you have help from an adult. Hot wax can be very dangerous.

WORD LIST

bodice: a tight-fitting top. Women wore them in the 1500s. They were often grand, with jewels and gold sewn into them. Later there was a kind of vest called a bodice.

breeches: a kind of trousers that reach just below the knees. They were the fashion for men from the 1600s to the 1800s.

buckskin: a kind of soft leather. It is made from the skin of a deer. The North American Indians used to make clothes from buckskin.

corset: tight underwear. People used to wear corsets to hold their stomachs in. They thought that corsets gave them better figures. Some people still wear them today.

cradle board: the North American Indians made these. They were like carry-cots. They were made of buckskin, on a wooden frame.

doublet: a padded jacket that men used to wear. Doublets were the fashion from the 1300s right through to the 1600s.

down: very soft feathers. People use down to make quilts and to make warm padded jackets for cold weather.

headdress: another word for any headgear, which isn't a hat. Headdresses are often worn for special occasions and may be highly decorated.

lace: a very pretty kind of trimming. It is made by arranging fine thread into patterns.

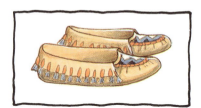

moccasins: traditional leather shoes made by North American Indians.

muff: a tube made from warm fabric. You put both hands inside a muff, to keep them warm.

nightcap: a hat you wear in bed at night. Nightcaps were often long and pointed.

oilskins: waterproof fabric. It is made using cloth and a kind of oil called linseed oil.

pads: a cushion of fabric. People wear pads and padded clothing to protect them in rough sports. We also use padded clothes to keep us warm in cold weather.

petticoat: a piece of underwear. It is a skirt you wear under a dress or a proper skirt.

sari: the traditional clothes that women from India wear. A sari is a long strip of beautiful cloth.

sequins: small pieces of glitter. People sew sequins on to clothes as decorations.

slops: puffed-out pants. They were the fashion for men in the 1500s. Men wore them with long stockings.

tunic: a piece of loose clothing, a bit like a shirt. Tunics are very simple garments. They usually have no fastenings: they slip over the head and cover the top half of the body.

uniform: when a group of people all have to wear the same kind of clothes, we say they are wearing a uniform. Nurses, sailors and the police all wear uniforms.

INDEX

The **dark** numbers tell you where you will find a picture of the subject.